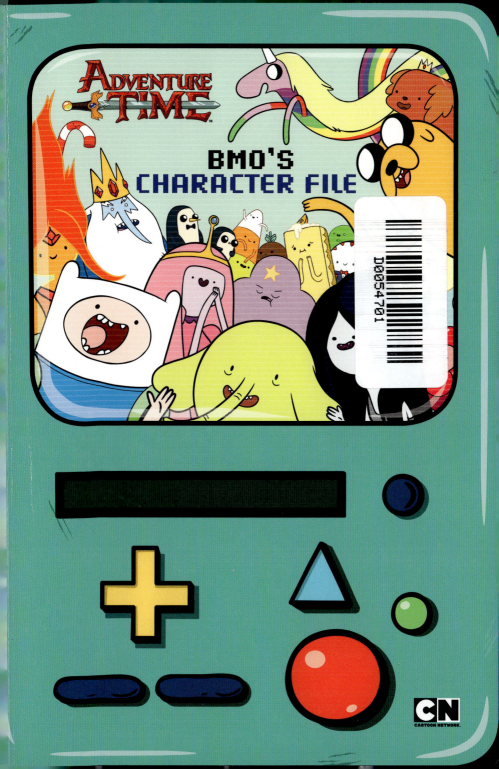

ISBN 978-0-8431-8012-1

EAN

5 0 6 9 9 >

BMO'S
CHARACTER FILE

by Brandon T. Snider

PSS!
PRICE STERN SLOAN
An Imprint of Penguin Group (USA) LLC

PRICE STERN SLOAN
Published by the Penguin Group
Penguin Group (USA) LLC
375 Hudson Street, New York, New York 10014, USA

USA | Canada | UK | Ireland | Australia | New Zealand | India | South Africa | China

penguin.com
A Penguin Random House Company

Published in 2014 by Price Stern Sloan, a division of Penguin Young Readers
Group, 345 Hudson Street, New York, New York 10014. PSS! is a registered
trademark of Penguin Group (USA) LLC. Printed in the USA.

ISBN 978-0-8431-8012-1   10 9 8 7 6 5 4 3 2 1

ADVENTURE TIME

There are so many different people in the Land of Ooo, and I am going to teach you all about them! My name is **BMO**, and I am a robot. First you have to guess what time it is. Are you ready? Okay. What time is it? **ANSWER: ADVENTURE TIME!** Ha-ha. That was funny. Now it's time for FUN!

—**BMO**

NAME: BMO

SPECIES: Robot Model 110 VOLT/60 HERTZ SYSTEM

ALIASES: B-Unit, Professor Pink

HAIR COLOR: I do not have hair, you silly goose.

STRENGTH: Being a friend to Finn and Jake!

WEAKNESS: I do not like being chafed, and I do not like to see good friends fight.

SPECIAL MOVE: BMO Chop!

BATTLE CRY: "Who wants to play video games?"

BIOGRAPHY: I am fun-loving and enjoy playing music for my friends Finn and Jake. They are really awesome guys. Skateboarding is also very fun. I love to have my circuits tickled, but that is a secret. Hee-hee. Let's take some nice pictures!

BIGGEST SECRET: New batteries make me feel *really* good.

ADDITIONAL QUOTE: "I'm awesome, boyee!"

SECRET JOB: Detective

FUN FACT: I love bread and butter.

FUN FACT: I can dance the worm!

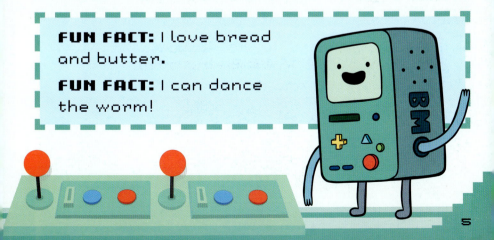

NAME: FINN THE HUMAN

SPECIES: Human

ALIASES: The Human, Davey, Prince Hot Bod, Finn Mertens

HAIR COLOR: Blond

STRENGTH: An awesome imagination and sense of adventure, duh!

WEAKNESS: He pees his pants constantly.

SPECIAL MOVE: There is a pranking demon that lives in his armpits.

BATTLE CRY: "I . . . am . . . complicated!"

BIOGRAPHY: Finn is a master of reality and a builder of pillow forts. His best friend and brother is Jake the Dog. Together they are lovable rascals who follow their hearts wherever they may take them. Nothing can stop Finn when he is on a crazy adventure, except maybe a noodle break.

ADDITIONAL QUOTE:
"What is this grib-a-grab?!"

BIGGEST SECRET: He loves to spend private time with a clump of Princess Bubblegum's hair.

FAVORITE INSTRUMENT: The flute

FAVORITE FOOD: Meatloaf

BIGGEST FEAR: The ocean

NAME: JAKE THE DOG

SPECIES: Dog

ALIASES: The Dog, Randy Butternubs,
Sir Jake: Baron of the Grasslands

HAIR COLOR: Mustard Yellow

STRENGTH: Stretchy Powers

WEAKNESS: Sometimes he does not cry
because he is afraid of feeling real emotions.

SPECIAL MOVE: He can play the viola very well. He is also a good fighter.

BATTLE CRY: "Get your hero on, dude!"

BIOGRAPHY: Jake is a dog. He is also Finn's brother and best friend in the entire universe. He uses his imagination to twist himself into a lot of cool shapes. Sometimes he wears pants made from spiderwebs (by tiny pixies). His girlfriend is Lady Rainicorn. They have five pups whom he loves very much.

FAVORITE TYPE OF HAND: Key Hand

FUN FACT: Jake was once eaten by a giant baby!

FAVORITE GAME: Slappin' the Jowls

NAME: ICE KING

SPECIES: Wizard (formerly human)

ALIASES: Ol' Frosty Knuckles, Señor Crybaby, Simon Petrikov

HAIR COLOR: White

STRENGTH: Losing himself in the Imagination Zone.

WEAKNESS: Princess Bubblegum's beautiful smile (and hair!)

SPECIAL MOVE: Kidnapping princesses.

BATTLE CRY: "By the power of ice and snow!"

BIOGRAPHY: Ice King was once a human scientist who found a magical crown that turned him into a cranky old wizard who doesn't have any friends. Aw, this is very sad for him. Maybe he would have more friends if he didn't kidnap people so much?

FUN FACT: Ice King loves to take artful photos of Gunter's body parts.

BIGGEST INSECURITY: His gross, old skin.

BIGGEST SECRET: He used to wear glasses.

ADDITIONAL QUOTE: "You get the squirty squirt squirts!"

A CREEPY THING: He falls asleep with his eyes open.

NAME: MARCELINE ABADEER

SPECIES: Vampire

ALIASES: The Vampire Queen, Tamer of Goldfish Beasts, Marcy

HAIR COLOR: Black

STRENGTH: She can shred on a guitar like you wouldn't believe.

WEAKNESS: Sunlight.

SPECIAL MOVE: She can raise an undead army.

BATTLE CRY: "Vampire Kick!"

BIOGRAPHY: Marceline is a vampire girl who can turn into a bat when she gets angry. Please do not make her angry, okay? Because she is a tortured soul, she has five hundred years of journals that she uses to write music. She loves to make music, especially after she gets into fights with her evil dad. It cheers her up!

FAVORITE COLOR: Red

FUN FACT: Marceline is a necromancer, which means she can raise the dead.

NAME: PRINCESS BONNIBEL BUBBLEGUM

SPECIES: Candy Person

ALIASES: P-Bubs, Peebs, Lady Quietbottom

HAIR COLOR: Pink

STRENGTH: She's a super smarty-pants at science.

WEAKNESS: Her heart hurts when she sees someone in trouble.

SPECIAL MOVE: Her crown and earrings have mysterious abilities. Ooo-Ooo!

BATTLE CRY: "What the nuts!?"

BIOGRAPHY: Princess Bubblegum can do just about anything that she puts her mind to! Not only does she speak many languages but she's also a very crafty inventor of cool stuff like Liquid Pyrotechnics. Best of all, she is nice and sweet to all of her royal subjects in the Candy Kingdom. Her favorite things are fun and mystery.

BEST ADVICE: "Don't be a butt!"

ADDITIONAL QUOTE: "This is dirt balls!"

FUN FACT: She is not really nineteen.

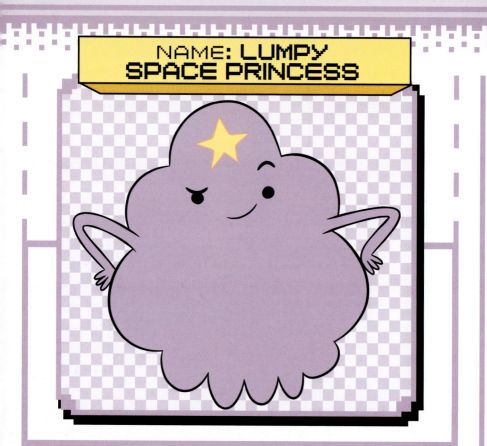

NAME: LUMPY SPACE PRINCESS

SPECIES: Lumpy Space Person

ALIASES: LSP, Lumpy, Sasspertina Lumpkins

HAIR COLOR: None (she has purple lumpiness instead)

STRENGTH: Floating and being rude

WEAKNESS: DO NOT ASK HER ABOUT BRAD, OKAY?!

SPECIAL MOVE: If she bites you then you'll become lumpy, too.

BATTLE CRY: "Oh my glob!"

BIOGRAPHY: Lumpy Space Princess can be not-so-nice sometimes. She likes to boss people around and make them do what she wants just because she is royalty. When people hear her coming they run and hide because she's so rude. I guess she probably makes fun of people because she is insecure. Oh well!

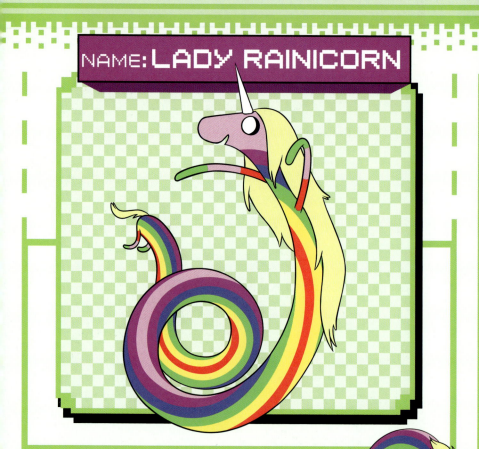

NAME: LADY RAINICORN

SPECIES: Rainicorn

ALIASES: Wind Rider, Lady R, Love Bugicorn

HAIR COLOR: Blond

STRENGTH: A beautiful and sleek rainicorn body, of course

WEAKNESS: Sometimes it is hard to understand what she says.

SPECIAL MOVE: Every day at 4 p.m. she has a date with her boyfriend, Jake the Dog. Awwww!

BATTLE CRY: "미안해요. 내가 국수를 너무 많이 먹었나 봐요."

BIOGRAPHY: Lady Rainicorn is a wonderful mixture of a unicorn and a rainbow. Her best friend is Princess Bubblegum, and they go on exciting adventures together. When she isn't busy gliding through the air she enjoys playing the viola and is very good at it (if you can believe it). She and her boyfriend, Jake, have five pups.

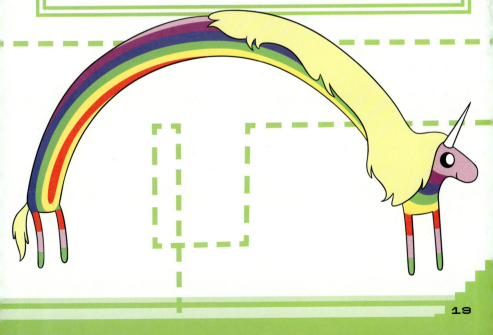

SPECIES: Elephant

ALIAS: Tee Tee

HAIR COLOR: Beautifully bald

STRENGTH: Kindness, honesty, and baking warm and delicious apple pies.

WEAKNESS: The Crystal Gem Apple.

SPECIAL MOVE: If you cross her, she will sass you something nasty!

BATTLE CRY: "I'm just a cute little elephant. I'm not cut out for adventuring."

BIOGRAPHY: Tree Trunks is the cutest little elephant lady you can ever imagine. She is sweet just like her world-famous apple pies. When she isn't having a tea party she enjoys collecting holographic stickers and stickers that smell like pickles. Don't you want to put her in your pocket?

FUN FACT: She does not like flies on her pies.

NAME: PIG

SPECIES: Pig
ALIASES: Mr. Pig, Piggy, Love Pig
HAIR COLOR: Pink
STRENGTH: He has super pig hearing.
WEAKNESS: He'd do anything for his little dove (Tree Trunks).
SPECIAL MOVE: Sometimes he has to eat criminals. Is that special?
BATTLE CRY: "When I see you, my heart beats like a choo-choo train. When you stand near me, I get so nervous I cannot move."
BIOGRAPHY: Pig is Tree Trunk's husband and they often have steamy times where everyone says, "Oh, that's gross! Please stop making all those kisses on each other!" But when you love someone you want to do that kind of stuff. Pig also does not have a home, so he has to "do what he has to do" to stay alive.

NAME: **EARL OF LEMONGRAB**

SPECIES: Candy Person

ALIASES: Limoncello, Count Lemon, Le Comte de la Citronnelle

HAIR COLOR: Yellow

STRENGTH: His lanky lemon body can withstand a lot of injury and he remembers EVERYTHING.

WEAKNESS: Has a hard time accepting things.

SPECIAL MOVE: Watch out because his sword is crazy powerful.

BATTLE CRY: "Unacceptable! One hundred years in the dungeon!"

BIOGRAPHY: The Earl of Lemongrab is one of Princess Bubblegum's experiments gone wrong, and he is very angry about it. He tried to take over the Candy Kingdom, but now he spends his time being mean to people and yelling a lot. Oh, and he does not know where food comes from, which is super weird, right?

FUN FACT: He has a favorite doll called Lemon-Sweets!

FUN FACT: Squeeze his head and juice comes out!

NAME: GUNTER

SPECIES: Penguin

ALIASES: Gundy, Gunder, Gunthy

HAIR COLOR: Black and white feathers

STRENGTH: A hot bod and a sparkling personality.

WEAKNESS: Breaking bottles.

SPECIAL MOVE: Making it all look so easy.

BATTLE CRY: "Wenk!"

BIOGRAPHY: When Gunter isn't being photographed by her master, the Ice King, she enjoys light conversation, obeying orders, and dancing into the night. She is a curious spirit who loves glamour in addition to marching in a straight line with her brothers Gunther, Goonter, and Günder. Gunter also has the honor of being the most evil thing that Hunson Abadeer has ever seen.

NAME: BILLY

SPECIES: Heroic Wanderer

ALIASES: Bill, William, Mister Hero

HAIR COLOR: Long white beard

STRENGTH: He is crazy-strong like a big hulking guy.

WEAKNESS: Violence. He does not like it at all.

SPECIAL MOVE: His sword Nothung will show you who the boss is!

BATTLE CRY: "I don't wanna buy anything!"

BIOGRAPHY: Who's the greatest warrior ever? A hero of renown! Who slayed an Evil Ocean? Who cast the Lich King down? Billy! And that time the evil Fire Count captured a damsel fair? Who saved her with such brav'ry, she offered him her hair? Billy! Also . . . he fought a bear! Billy!

NAME: HUNSON ABADEER

SPECIES: Demon

ALIASES: Lord of Evil, Hunny Bear, Dark Ruler of the Nightosphere

HAIR COLOR: Black

STRENGTH: He is very flexible.

WEAKNESS: He has a soft spot in his heart for his daughter, Marceline.

SPECIAL MOVE: His evil Nightosphere amulet will suck your soul out of your body when you're not watching. Oh, and the Karate Kick.

BATTLE CRY: "You can't destroy me!"

BIOGRAPHY: Hunson Abadeer is a very, very bad dark guy who uses his meanie powers to cause all sorts of trouble. He's so wicked that he once ate his daughter Marceline's french fries.  Can you believe the nerve of him? Also, his teeth are sharp and scary, so just stay away from him from now on, okay?

SPECIES: Lich

ALIASES: Lich King, L-Drizzle, Lichy Lichy Coco Pop

HAIR COLOR: What's under that horned helmet is anybody's guess.

STRENGTH: Green flame-y powers, mind control, and leaving a trail of death.

WEAKNESS: The Gauntlet of the Hero and any type of amber prison.

SPECIAL MOVE: Using the Well of Power to possess poor souls like Princess Bubblegum.

BATTLE CRY: "You are a joke . . . to me!"

BIOGRAPHY: The Lich is really evil. He is really, really evil. Under all those layers of clothing is the heart of a very bad guy—like, the worst. The Lich wishes to destroy all life and plunge the world into darkness. It's very important that everyone shine as bright as possible to make sure he doesn't!

FINN AND JAKE'S FAMILY

NAME: Joshua

SPECIES: Dog

SPECIAL MOVE: He used to make pickles for Jake and his brothers!

BATTLE CRY: "I said hurt everyone *that is evil*. Let me finish next time."

BIOGRAPHY: Joshua is Finn and Jake's dad who is a little rough around the edges. Or, because he is a dog, you can say "ruff" around the edges as a joke. Ha-ha. He loves his family, even though he makes his sons fight. He says it will toughen them up. Who knows? They seem very tough already.

NAME: Margaret

SPECIES: Dog

SPECIAL MOVE: She always knew the right thing to say when Finn and Jake were feeling sad.

BATTLE CRY: "Get that book out of your mouth!"

BIOGRAPHY: Margaret was Finn and Jake's sweet mother who took care of them and their brothers a long time ago, back when they were little. She gave her kids as much love as possible because that's what mommy dogs do. She even used to sing sweet lullaby songs to help them sleep. Awwwww.

NAME: Jermaine

SPECIES: Dog

SPECIAL MOVE: Being able to forgive Jake for stuff that happened in the past.

BATTLE CRY: "Yo, that was an accident, I knew you were just horsin' off!"

BIOGRAPHY: Jermaine is Finn and Jake's brother. He looks just like Jake except that Jermaine has a flabby belly and is missing some teeth. They are very close in age and used to be good pals until Jake did a bad thing to Jermaine. But please don't worry about their friendship. They worked everything out, and now they are all good!

NAME: SNAIL

SPECIES: Snail

ALIAS: The Lich

HAIR COLOR: None

STRENGTH: Snail is everywhere!

WEAKNESS: Sometimes Snail is really the Lich!

SPECIAL MOVE: Snail can be really tricky and hide where you do not think to look.

BATTLE CRY: "Yessss . . . One step closer."

BIOGRAPHY: Snail is totally a low-key kind of guy but then he was possessed by the Lich and had evil green eyes and a mean look on his face. This was not good. But now he is back to being himself. Sometimes he is sitting on a leaf and sometimes he is sitting on your back. Variety is spicy!

NAME: **CAPTAIN BANANA GUARD**
AND THE **BANANA GUARDS**

SPECIES: Candy People

ALIASES: Commander Plantain and the Plátanos

HAIR COLOR: Chocolate!

STRENGTH: Guarding

WEAKNESS: Flavored milk.

SPECIAL MOVE: If you get trapped in their B formation, you're in big trouble.

BATTLE CRY: "Halt!"

BIOGRAPHY: Captain Banana Guard and his loyal Banana Guards protect Princess Bubblegum and her magical castle from harm. There are so many of these guys that it is very difficult to tell them apart. Sometimes I see a Banana Guard and think, "That's my friend Phil!" but really it is not. They should dress differently sometimes for fun.

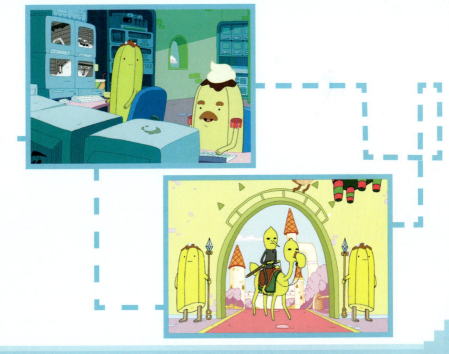

NAME: COSMIC OWL

ALIAS: C. Owl

HAIR COLOR: Awesome gold and brown feathers

STRENGTH: Cosmic Owl has all the awesomest board games.

WEAKNESS: Speak up because his hearing is not so good.

SPECIAL MOVE: This is a big secret. Don't tell. Here it is in invisible ink:

BATTLE CRY: "You're a sociopath."

BIOGRAPHY: There is so much mystery about Cosmic Owl, but even so, he is a really chill, cool dude who likes hanging out when he is not the master of the galaxy. He loves to have party time, munch on tasty snacks, and if there is a hot tub nearby he will relax in it with you like a true bro. Aw man, I like this guy.

NAME: PRISMO

SPECIES: Celestial Being

ALIAS: Guardian of the Time Room

HAIR COLOR: None (he has a puffy pink head shadow)

STRENGTH: Having a cool TV wall that plays whatever you want.

WEAKNESS: He gets a little lonely at nighttime.

SPECIAL MOVE: Once you taste Prismo's homemade artisanal pickles, your life will be different.

BATTLE CRY: "Nah-Nah-Nah-Nah-Nasty! Nasty jazz!"

BIOGRAPHY: If you walk into Prismo's Time Room he will give you one wish that he will make come true. Be very specific, because it will have an ironic twist. He does not do this to be mean, he does it to be funny, even though it might not always be. He said his friends are nasty. It was funny. Ha-ha!

THE RAINICORNS!

NAME: Bob Rainicorn (Lady Rainicorn's father) and Ethel Rainicorn (Lady Rainicorn's mother)

SPECIES: Rainicorns

ALIASES: Mom and Dad

HAIR COLOR: Blond

STRENGTH: They love their daughter, Lady Rainicorn, SO MUCH!

WEAKNESS: They are a little blind.

SPECIAL MOVE: When they turn on their Universal Translator everyone can understand what they are saying.

BATTLE CRY: "We're about ready to break out our picnic basket and dig in!" —Bob; "Oh, oh! Let's play some traditional Rainicorn games!" —Ethel

BIOGRAPHY: Bob and Ethel Rainicorn live at 47 Rainbow Street and are very humble Rainicorns who like life's simple pleasures. They were very happy when their daughter, Lady Rainicorn, met Jake the Dog. They are accepting of him because Bob was saved by a dog in the Rainicorn-Dog Wars. War is not fun.

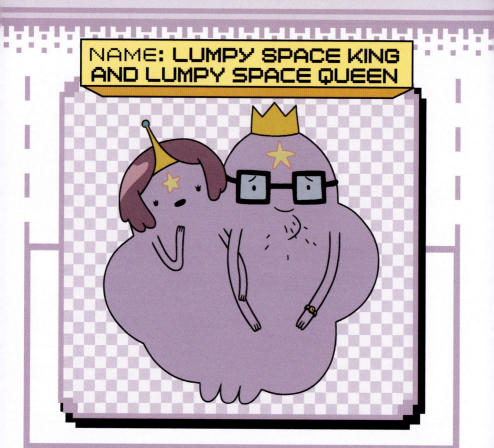

SPECIES: Lumpy Space People

ALIASES: LSK and LSQ

HAIR COLOR: None

STRENGTH: They are tough but loving parents.

WEAKNESS: When Lumpy Space People get married, their bodies are attached to each other forever.

SPECIAL MOVE: Lump shifts

BATTLE CRY: "You've made your mother cry for the last time, daughter! You are hereby banned from using the Royal Car!" —Lumpy Space King; "What did you just say?! What did you just say?!" —Lumpy Space Queen

BIOGRAPHY: Lumpy Space King is overprotective of his daughter, Lumpy Space Princess. He does not like her hanging out with smooth people and driving the Royal Car. But then Lumpy Space Queen calms him down and says, "It will all be okay!" That is what good couples that love each other do.

NAME: PARTY PAT

SPECIES: Bear

ALIASES: The Chief, HBIC
(Head Bear in Charge), Pat

HAIR COLOR: Brown

STRENGTH: This guy knows how to party,
have fun, and dance all night.

WEAKNESS: He is addicted to honey-
flavored energy drinks.

SPECIAL MOVE: Break dancing!

BATTLE CRY: "Before you talk to the Chief, you must party with the Chief. It is the only way."

BIOGRAPHY: Party Pat is kind of quiet and dresses very hip, but he can live it up like a million rock stars. His colorful bear friends are so crazy that they once partied all night in a monster's belly. Having fun is a way of life for these guys. I wonder when they will stop and have a nap. Maybe never.

SPECIES: Fire Elemental

ALIAS: Flambit No. 1

HAIR COLOR: Flamey orange!

STRENGTH: When someone is up to no good, he will tell you so you can stop them.

WEAKNESS: Water (and a girly scream)!

SPECIAL MOVE: Nothing gets by his flame shields, so don't even try it, buddy!

BATTLE CRY: "Come on, you know I'm on the level!"

BIOGRAPHY: Flambo talks kind of funny like he is a tough guy, but inside his fire heart is a good boy. If you need something to be flamey, he will light it on fire with no problems at all. See? That is what a nice person would do, not a bad person. But he can also be a rascal like Finn and Jake, so be careful.

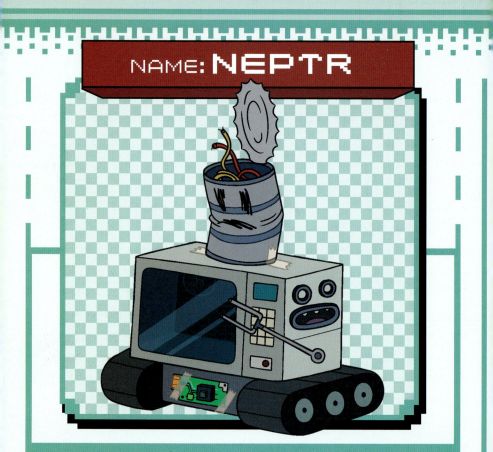

SPECIES: Robot

ALIASES: Never-Ending Pie-Throwing Robot, Nep, Ultimate Hide-and-Seek Champion

HAIR COLOR: None

STRENGTH: Throwing pies.

WEAKNESS: He can't play video games or shoot lasers.

SPECIAL MOVE: If things get too hot he can create fireproof suits for protection, so that's good.

BATTLE CRY: "NEPTR loves you, creator!"

BIOGRAPHY: It was so funny that one time when Finn built NEPTR out of a trash heap just to prank Jake by throwing a pie at him. Ha-ha. But then he still hung around, which is okay, but he can be annoying sometimes when he wants to hang out. It's a good thing the Ice King treats him like a son or he'd never leave.

NAME: **FLAME PRINCESS**

SPECIES: Fire Elemental

ALIASES: Flamey P, Princess of Flames, Gloria, FP

HAIR COLOR: Orange flames

STRENGTH: She can create fireballs and turn people into fire and fire, fire, fire!

WEAKNESS: Water, rain, wet stuff, puddles.

SPECIAL MOVE: Her Flame Sword is awesome.

BATTLE CRY: "Do the splits, thou milk-livered maggot pie!"

BIOGRAPHY: Flame Princess is an unstoppable force of destruction, so her daddy kept her in a bottle. But that's not very nice to do even though she is kind of crazy. Her powers make it hard to find friends because no one wants to get burned. One time Finn cried soft, wet tears that hurt her skin. It was sad.

NAME: THE PRINCESSES OF THE LAND OF OOO

BIOGRAPHY: There are so many fancy princesses in the Land of Ooo that it is hard to keep track of them all. Every day, a new one pops up and says hello. They are like flowers blooming in the springtime.

NAME: Hot Dog Princess

SPECIAL MOVE: She smells like old hot-dog water (and has a crush on Finn).

BATTLE CRY: "Thank you so much, Finn! I should give you a kiss!"

NAME: Engagement Ring Princess

SPECIAL MOVE: She might trick you into marrying her.

BATTLE CRY: "Did I tell you that I like the opera? But if you don't, I hate it!"

NAME: Breakfast Princess and Toast Princess

SPECIAL MOVE: Ruling the Breakfast Kingdom together!

BATTLE CRY: "Oh yeah, that would be great, thanks." —Breakfast Princess

NAME: Skeleton Princess

SPECIAL MOVE: Her skirt is made out of dead birds.

BATTLE CRY: "[Grumbling.]"

NAME: Cotton Candy Princess

SPECIAL MOVE: If you save her life she might give you some of her hair.

NAME: Elbow Princess

SPECIAL MOVE: Even though she is missing part of her hip, she can still shake her booty.

NAME: Emerald Princess

SPECIAL MOVE: It is a mystery!

NAME: Desert Princess

SPECIAL MOVE: She can make sand into people!

NAME: Wildberry Princess

SPECIAL MOVE: She can remove all the berries from her body if she wants.

BATTLE CRY: "Oh no, this is a medical condition. I need a hospital."

NAME: Muscle Princess

SPECIAL MOVE: Just look at her body. She could crush you with her pinkie finger.

BATTLE CRY: "If I had beautiful shiny hair, no one would look at my muscles! Come back when you want to get serious about loving me!"

NAME: Princess Monster-Wife

SPECIAL MOVE: She has a very good heart inside her crazy patchwork body.

BATTLE CRY: "You'd love me even without these other princesses' parts?"

NAME: Old Lady Princess

SPECIAL MOVE: It's very easy to control her mind. Actually, that is not good at all.

BATTLE CRY: "You lousy, butt-faced pig! I hate you!"

NAME: Turtle Princess

SPECIAL MOVE: She is head of the library! Mmmmmm, books.

NAME: Embryo Princess

SPECIAL MOVE: Her telekinetic power protects her in a fun, pinky bubble.

NAME: Bounce House Princess

SPECIAL MOVE: Being a soft air bed that everyone can jump on!

NAME: Princess Princess Princess

SPECIAL MOVE: Look at this girl. She has a lot of special moves, I bet.

NAME: LUMPY SPACE PEOPLE

BIOGRAPHY: Lumpy Space People are kind of weird.

NAME: Brad

SPECIAL MOVE: Being the super ultimate love of Lumpy Space Princess's life.
BATTLE CRY: "Hey . . ."

NAME: Melissa

SPECIAL MOVE: She is Lumpy Space Princess's best friend, but now she is also dating Brad and it is very dramatic.
BATTLE CRY: "Tonight ith the weekly promcoming danthe!"

NAME: Monty

SPECIAL MOVE: He does not like to be a Lumpy Space Person at all.
BATTLE CRY: "A smoothie like you will plummet right into the eternal void."

NAME: Lenny

SPECIAL MOVE: Aw, he is a really nice guy. Hard to find, am I right, ladies? High-five!
BATTLE CRY: "Yeah, lumpiness sucks!"

NAME: Glasses

SPECIAL MOVE: There is something fishy with Glasses. Ha-ha this is another good joke for you.
BATTLE CRY: "I'd say there's a fifty-fifty chance of you making it."

NAME: Lumpy Space Messenger

SPECIAL MOVE: He is really the best at messengering.

NAME: Lumpy Space Prince

SPECIAL MOVE: He is just like Lumpy Space Princess, except for his light hairy mustache.

NAME: NUT PEOPLE

NAME: Duke of Nuts

SPECIAL MOVE: Poor guy cannot stop eating pudding. But at least he is dressed fancy-cool.

BATTLE CRY: "People make mistakes. It's all a part of growing up, and you never really stop growing."

NAME: Duchess of Nuts

SPECIAL MOVE: She is also fancy, because she can talk to nuts and hear what they say.

BATTLE CRY: "Would you like to hear what MY NUTS HAVE TO SAY?"

NAME: Marquis of Nuts

SPECIAL MOVE: He is crazy protective of his daddy, so be careful or he might yell at you.

BATTLE CRY: "No one will kill the Duke of Nuts! I will kill whoever seeks to arrest him!"

NAME: Peanut Baby

SPECIAL MOVE: He is good at napping and pooping and being a Peanut Baby.

BATTLE CRY: "Goo-goo, gaa-gaa!"

NAME: Lisby the Cashew Butler

SPECIAL MOVE: He is so fun and nice and the best butler of all time.

BATTLE CRY: "Why are you thinking so hard?! Just party hard! Whoo!"

NAME: JAKE AND LADY'S PUPPIES

SPECIES: Dog/Rainicorn

BIOGRAPHY: When Jake and Lady Rainicorn became boyfriend and girlfriend they were smoochy-woochy with each other. Now they have a litter of puppies! Together they are very protective of their family, sometimes a little too much. But it is okay, because they all love each other a lot. When all the pups come together they make one big super pup! OH BOY!

BATTLE CRY: "수학!" ("Mathematical!")

NAME: Charlie

STRENGTHS: She can fly and teleport from place to place.

NAME: T.V.

STRENGTHS: He can teleport but cannot fly because he is too plump.

NAME: Viola

STRENGTHS: She can change colors and fly using her tail as a propeller.

NAME: Jake Jr.

STRENGTHS: She can fly, teleport, and shape-shift using her funky hair.

NAME: Kim Kil Whan

STRENGTHS: He can fly, teleport, colorize stuff, and stretch his body into different shapes.

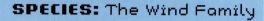

SPECIES: The Wind Family

ALIAS: Bubble

HAIR COLOR: Clear

STRENGTH: Without Air everything would die. He helps us live!

WEAKNESS: His memory gets all jumbled and he gets lost sometimes.

SPECIAL MOVE: Helping babies find their mommies.

BATTLE CRY: "I'm a bubble."

BIOGRAPHY: Bubble is always there to help when you get lost in the woods and need to get home! But he will say that he wants to marry you. This makes Jake pop him and act like a real buttdog. But there is good news! Bubble is now Air, and he is all around us forever and ever. This is a sweet love story.

NAME: SPARKLE

SPECIES: Giant Baby

ALIAS: Ricky

HAIR COLOR: None

STRENGTH: He is the most handsome baby in the woods. He is also flabby and hard to move.

WEAKNESS: Sometimes he does not want to eat his potato.

SPECIAL MOVE: Pooping in his diaper when no one is looking.

BATTLE CRY: "Waaaaaaaaah!"

BIOGRAPHY: The future is wide open to little Sparkle even though his name will always be Ricky in our hearts. Maybe he will grow up to be a hit man or a strapping horse whisperer? Sometimes his mommy needs to keep a better eye on him so he does not fall into a bucket of fire snakes.

NAME: LORRAINE

SPECIES: Chicken

ALIASES: Lorrainestorm, The Cluckinator, Cynthia

HAIR COLOR: Gray feathers

STRENGTH: Lorraine is red-hot like pizza supper.

WEAKNESS: She cannot resist the love of a good person.

SPECIAL MOVE: Taking someone's heart and stomping all over it.

BATTLE CRY: "Cluck?"

BIOGRAPHY: Lorraine is the kind of chicken that waltzes into your life and shows you how to live again. But you must be very careful, because she will destroy you from the inside out with her lies and deception. She is also very attractive, and I cannot stop thinking about her.

NAME: BEBE

SPECIES: Gadget

ALIASES: Clicky Clickerton, Dirty Bebe, the Controller

HAIR COLOR: Black plastic

STRENGTH: Stealing people's girlfriends.

WEAKNESS: Remove his batteries and he's a goner.

SPECIAL MOVE: Ironically pushing people's buttons.

BATTLE CRY: "Click!"

BIOGRAPHY: Bebe owns a dance club. It is called Bebe's because that is his name. He's a bad mamajama. Do not mess with him, because he is dangerous and rude and will probably steal from you. He yells at ladies, which makes him the king of the jerkwads. Stay away from him or you'll be sorry.

NAME: RONNIE

SPECIES: Rodent

ALIASES: Ron, Ronald, Ronda

HAIR COLOR: Gray

STRENGTH: Accusing people of murder even if they did not do it.

WEAKNESS: A lovely chicken.

SPECIAL MOVE: Not keeping his trap shut.

BATTLE CRY: "Squee?"

BIOGRAPHY: Ronnie lived in a Tree Fort and used to do all kinds of bad things like lying to people and framing them for murder. He just didn't know how to stay out of trouble and ended up paying the ultimate price for his crimes. Ronnie learned that justice comes in small packages.

NAME: JIGGLER

SPECIES: Jiggler

ALIASES: Jiggler?, Jiggler!, Ralph

HAIR COLOR: None

STRENGTH: The Toothbrush Dance

WEAKNESS: Being away from his mommy.

SPECIAL MOVE: He will eat a drawing right out of your hand if you let him.

BATTLE CRY: [A whistling sound.]

BIOGRAPHY: Jigglers are cute little dance machines that love to give out kisses. They're so sweet! When they're away from their mommy for too long they get very sick and start to puke up pink juice, which is cool to watch but very disgusting. Always make sure to take them back home so they can feel better.

NAME: FLAME KING

SPECIES: Fire Elemental

ALIAS: King of Fire

HAIR COLOR: Flamey orange

STRENGTH: He is a stern king of fire. Do not cross him or you will burn (this is a warning).

WEAKNESS: He loves his daughter very much, even though she runs away from him.

SPECIAL MOVE: Killing his brother to become king. Sheesh, this guy is not sweet like candy.

BATTLE CRY: "Silence, my molten mamas."

BIOGRAPHY: Flame King has a very bad temper, but he is a hothead so what do you expect? Ha-ha, just kidding—but no, really, he is a bad guy. Because he is a king he wants his way or the highway. His royal subjects have to do what he says or he will light a fire under them. Ha-ha, another joke—but it is true.

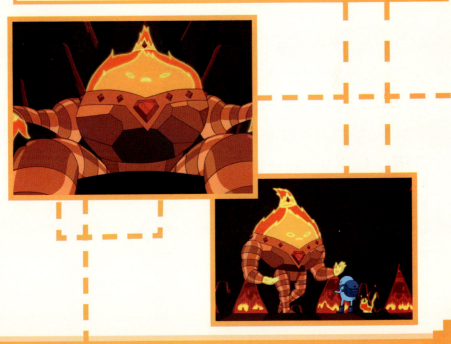

NAME: WIZARDS!

BIOGRAPHY: Oh, wow. There are so many wizards in the Land of Ooo. Like a bazillion gajillion!

NAME: Huntress Wizard

SPECIAL MOVE: She can shoot lightning bolts from her hands and she shoots magic arrows. Eeeee!

BATTLE CRY: "What's it look like, you donk?"

NAME: Wizard Thief

SPECIAL MOVE: He can turn into a cat and make swirly pink spells.

BATTLE CRY: "Pancake, pancake, pancake."

NAME: Science Whyzard

SPECIAL MOVE: *Shhhh!* She is actually Doctor Princess in disguise, but don't tell.

BATTLE CRY: "Whoa, Nelly! Something . . . medical is happening!"

NAME: Rock Wizard

SPECIAL MOVE: He does all kinds of rocky stuff with rocks and rocky rocks.

NAME: Dimension Wizard

SPECIAL MOVE: He can open up magical portals to other dimensions. Oh boy!

NAME: CANDY PEOPLE

BIOGRAPHY: Candy People are very sweet. Sometimes they are also sour. Ha-ha. These are more funny jokes.

NAME: Cinnamon Bun

SPECIAL MOVE: Awwww. Poor Cinnamon Bun. He should be called Clumsy Bun instead.

BATTLE CRY: "Okay. I'm gonna do it. Okay, okay, okay. Everyone watch! I'm gonna do a flip!"

NAME: Peppermint Butler

SPECIAL MOVE: Peppermint Butler is a good guy but very mysterious in his past. Ooo-Ooo.

BATTLE CRY: "I'd like your flesh."

NAME: Punchy

SPECIAL MOVE: This little smiling punch bowl is the life of the party forever and ever.

BATTLE CRY: "What a wonderful, marvelous party!"

NAME: Mr. Cupcake

SPECIAL MOVE: Wow, he has big, gigantic, huge muscles.
BATTLE CRY: "Do you prefer chocolate or fudge?"

NAME: Smudge

SPECIAL MOVE: He is a bad guy who is very good at guarding bodies.

NAME: Chocoberry

SPECIAL MOVE: She has a crush on Mr. Cupcake. Don't tell! (Everybody knows.)

NAME: Dr. Dextrose

SPECIAL MOVE: He is a doctor. All of his moves are special, silly dude.

NAME: Manfried

SPECIAL MOVE: A piñata that talks? Ha-ha. What will they think of next?

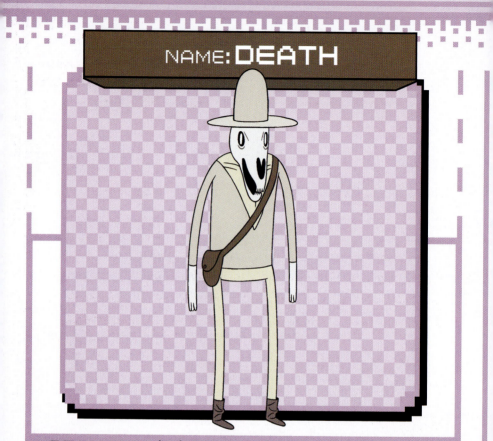

NAME: DEATH

SPECIES: Skeleton

ALIAS: Ruler of the Land of the Dead

HAIR COLOR: None

STRENGTH: He can make force fields and teleport. He is also a good drummer.

WEAKNESS: He does not like people who cheat him. Oh, he does not like them AT ALL.

SPECIAL MOVE: Beware his Kiss of Death! It is not a sweet kiss like you get from a lovey person. No way.

BATTLE CRY: "I'm going to kill you now."

BIOGRAPHY: Death is a like a scary cowboy that comes to town to scare you. If you see him come to your town, you should run away and never look back. His face looks like a horse and also a skull. He should be called Horse Face Skull Dude. Oh no! Don't tell him I said that, please.

NAME: SHELBY

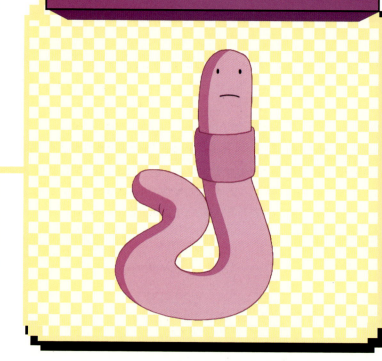

SPECIES: Earthworm

ALIAS: Just Shelby

HAIR COLOR: None

STRENGTH: Coming up with good ideas.

WEAKNESS: He doesn't hate thimbles of milk, but he doesn't love them either.

SPECIAL MOVE: He is the voice of reason when people need an extra bit of help.

BATTLE CRY: "Check, please."

BIOGRAPHY: Shelby is a simple earthworm who sometimes finds himself getting into adventures with his friends. He lives in Jake's viola, too, which is probably a fun place to live for an earthworm because it is small and has lots of room for him to move around. Shelby's voice is funny sometimes!

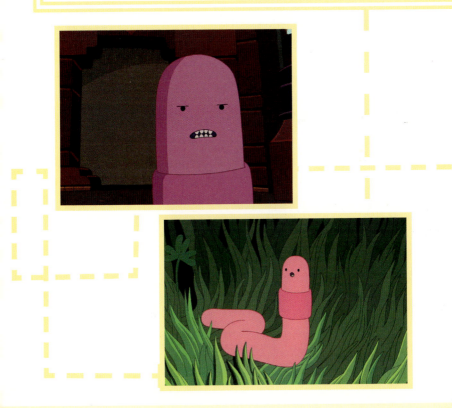

NAME: DONNY

SPECIES: Grass Ogre

ALIASES: Don, Donald, Donda

HAIR COLOR: Green

STRENGTH: Squeezing chickens

WEAKNESS: He will not tell anyone, so do not ask or he will get you.

SPECIAL MOVE: His body makes Obnoxygen, which is very special, to protect the House People.

BATTLE CRY: "YOU put on some pants!"

BIOGRAPHY: Donny's favorite things are being a jerkwad and drinking apple juice. Well, guess what. He is all out of apple juice! That was a joke. Sometimes they do not work. Donny wishes he could be nicer, but then the House People would get eaten by Why-Wolves, which is really bad.

SPECIES: Robot

ALIAS: Not BMO

HAIR COLOR: None

STRENGTH: Listening to BMO explain how to be pretty cool.

WEAKNESS: Still has so much to learn.

SPECIAL MOVE: Can hear the screaming squirrels.

BATTLE CRY: "I am not BMO!"

BIOGRAPHY: When Finn and Jake go adventuring, Football comes out to play! Football enjoys learning about tea parties and grapefruit spoons. No one can know about Football, so please hush if someone asks.